# Living a Holy Life
# A Biblical Survey

Samson Namala

ISBN 978-1-68570-578-7 (paperback)
ISBN 978-1-68570-579-4 (digital)

Christian Faith Publishing, Inc.
832 Park Avenue
Meadville, PA 16335
www.christianfaithpublishing.com

Printed in the United States of America

# Contents

# Acknowledgment

I am grateful to the Lord Almighty for choosing Sundar Rao Namala and Deiva Krupa Rao Namala to be my parents even before the foundation of the world and for saving them at a young age. They were role models for me in learning how to live a godly life and to depend on the Lord in every circumstance.

I am thankful and grateful to the Lord for the testimonies of Pastor Bruce Boehmer and Brother Ebenezer Gujjarlapudi. God used these brothers in Christ to train me in several aspects of ministry like teaching, building relationships, and serving.

# Scripture

[13]Therefore, preparing your minds for action,[b] and being sober-minded, set your hope fully on the grace that will be brought to you at the revelation of Jesus Christ. [14]As obedient children, do not be conformed to the passions of your former ignorance, [15]but as he who called you is holy, you also be holy in all your conduct, [16]since it is written, "You shall be holy, for I am holy." [17]And if you call on him as Father who judges impartially according to each one's deeds, conduct yourselves with fear throughout the time of your exile, [18]knowing that you were ransomed from the futile ways inherited from your forefathers, not with perishable things such as silver or gold, [19]but with the precious blood of Christ, like that of a lamb without blemish or spot. [20]He was foreknown before the foundation of the world but was made manifest in the last times for the sake of you [21]who through him are believers in God, who raised him from the dead and gave him glory, so that your faith and hope are in God.

[22]Having purified your souls by your obedience to the truth for a sincere brotherly love, love one another earnestly from a pure heart. (1 Peter 1:13–22 ESV)

# Introduction

There are numerous perceptions and misconceptions on what it really means to be holy. I was born into a strong Christian family. My parents were actively involved in serving God even before my birth. Due to their involvement in ministry, I had the opportunity to watch my parents closely and understood what it means to be holy—by their way of life. Their disciplines, priorities, choices, words, and interactions were distinctly different from others. Right from my childhood, I understood that my parents were dedicated to pleasing the Lord in every aspect of their lives. When I was a child, there were more than a few occasions where I observed my father reading scripture and meditating long before the sun had risen. After his private devotions, he would gather the family for a time of family prayer. My dad was an executive in the private industry while my mother served the family as a homemaker. The days that I was home from school, I witnessed my mother spend hours reading the Word of God and in prayer during the course of the day. Often ladies from our church would come to our house to visit mom and spend time in prayer. Most evenings my parents were either at church or visiting someone in need. My parents would always end each day with family prayer, even though it would be much later in the day, after they returned from church. The format of our family prayer was similar to a worship service. It involved worship through songs, reading the Word, and having each family member pray. When I was growing up as a child in India, a typical workweek was six days with Sunday being the only day off. As such, after a week of busyness with schooling, Sunday was the busiest day of the week for us, which, most often than not, meant we would spend all day at church.

When other itinerant pastors would come to either minister at our church or stay at our house, I witnessed a similar lifestyle. I would notice that the pastor (and sometimes their family came to our home) would spend most of the day in prayer and reading God's Word. They were humble people whose lives revolved around serving God and His work. Their conversations revolved around God and His faithfulness.

Growing up as a kid, I thought that living an austere life like those I witnessed in my parents and the itinerant pastors is what made people holy. I quickly realized there is no way I can attain that level of holiness. What I failed to understand was that this kind of austere living was a result of being "internally holy." This type of lifestyle does not have the ability to make a person holy.

Most people have misconceptions about what it means to be holy. People often equate performance of "good works" to being holy. There are several delusions about holiness. Some opine that a person becomes holy based on the acts of charity they've performed. Some state that we can attain a level of holiness by contributing our wealth and time to religious activities. Some believe that people who do better as compared to bad qualify them as holy people. There are others who are of the opinion that going to a religious place regularly and doing acts of piety will make a person holy. There are others who opine that pilgrimage to a particular sacred place will make a person holy.

However, in the grand scheme of things, it really does not matter how we define or what we think of holiness. It matters what the ultimate standard of "holiness" is. And that is God. So the ultimate question is, "What does God say about holiness?" In order to be acceptable to God, we need to have a true understanding of holiness based on who God is and what He has declared as being holy in His presence.

The first place to begin to understand holiness is by studying the character of God. The Scripture reveals who God is. In the Scriptures, the sovereign God reveals Himself as self-existing (Exodus 3:14), glorious (Exodus 24:17), merciful (Exodus 34:6), consuming fire (Deuteronomy 4:24), jealous (Deuteronomy 4:24), faithful (Deuteronomy 7:9), "God of gods" and "Lords of lords" (Deuteronomy 10:17), righteous (Deuteronomy 32:4), a rock (2

Samuel 22:32), almighty (Job 11:7), perfect (Psalm 18:30), good (Psalm 34:8), a shield (Psalm 84:11), gracious (Psalm 116:5), great (Psalm 147:5), omnipresent (Jeremiah 23:24), compassionate (Micah 7:19), unchanging (Malachi 3:6), spirit (John 4:24), wise (Romans 16:27), peace (2 Thessalonians 3:16) eternal (1 Timothy 1:17), patient (2 Peter 3:9), light (1 John 1:5), love (1 John 4:8), and holy (Revelation 4:8).

Among all the self-revelations of God, only His holiness is emphasized in Scripture as "Holy, Holy, Holy" (Isaiah 6:3). Scripture emphasizes this character so that we clearly understand how holy God is. No other characteristic is emphasized as His Holiness, which gives us insight into His character and being.

When Prophet Isaiah was granted a vision of the person and glory of God, he was privileged to witness heavenly worship first-hand. He saw the Lord seated on the throne, high and uplifted. There were six seraphim calling out to each other and crying out, "Holy, holy, holy is the Lord of hosts; the whole earth is full of His glory" (Isaiah 6:3). That was about in 740 BC. In the last book of the Bible, John the apostle was ushered into the throne room of God. There he witnessed heavenly worship. John records that he saw God seated on the throne. On each side of the throne were four living creatures. They were worshipping the Lord day and night without ceasing, saying, "Holy, holy, holy is the Lord God Almighty, who was and is and is to come!" (Revelation 4:8). This was about AD 95. We see two godly men witness worship in heaven about 834 years apart, and the subject of worship revolved around the absolute holiness of God. Heaven is enthralled with the holiness of God.

Holiness is the only essential trait or nature of God, which is repeated thrice while describing God. We know that God is holy. On the other hand, we live in a fallen and sinful world. We are born in sin. From our childhood, we remember the many sins we committed. Most of the time, if not ever, our parents or any others did not encourage us to sin. On the contrary, we willingly disobeyed and committed many other offenses against God and others. As we grow, we grow also in our sinfulness because of our sinful nature. But God is unlike us. As a holy God, there is no hint of evil, sin, or darkness in Him.

Such a God commands us to be holy. In 1 Peter 1:16, Apostle Peter repeats a command from the old testament that says, "You shall be holy, for I am holy." When I encounter this scripture, I am rendered hopeless and helpless. There is no way I can do anything to comply with this impossible imperative from the holy God. There is no way I can be holy to any standard that is commanded in Scripture. When we read the Bible, we are quite often left in a quandary as we often find that God's Word is easy to read and sometimes understand but almost impossible to perfectly obey.

However, God has not left us to figure out how we can strive to obey and thereby grow in holiness. In the Bible, 1 Peter 1: 13–22 provides practical instructions on how we can lead a holy life through the empowering work of the Holy Spirit. Apostle Peter presents seven disciplines that enable us to grow in holiness. Steven Covey wrote a book published in 1989 called *The Seven Habits of Highly Effectively People*. This book went on to become one of the best sellers. This book describes seven habits that, when incorporated into one's life, can help them be successful. In this passage, Peter is giving us seven practical behaviors that, if we ask for God's help and prayerfully follow, can help us grow in holiness before God. Before we discover what these disciplines may be, it is good for us to understand the standard of holiness that God desires.

The word *hágios* is the most frequently used word in the original to describe the concept of holiness in the Bible. The word means to be set apart, primarily for use in divine service. Even in this fallen and sinful world, there are certain things that God desires for His people to consider holy or set apart. In the Old Testament, God refers to the place as the holy ground where the Lord appeared to Moses (Exodus 3:5), Sabbath day as a holy day (Exodus 20:8), the garments made for priests as holy garments (Exodus 28:2, 4), the nation of Israel as a holy nation (Deuteronomy 7:6), and the vessels used in the house of God as holy vessels (Ezra 8:28). A thing becomes holy in the sight of God when it is set apart by God to be used by God for His glory and purpose.

When it comes to holiness, Scripture primarily presents two elements: positional holiness and practical holiness. Any individual is considered positionally holy in the sight of God the moment they are converted (Holiness: Pitfalls, Struggles, & Victory by David Cloud). As the Bible makes it clear: every individual born into this world is a sinner (Romans 3:23), and without holiness, no man or woman can see God (Hebrews 12:14).

The wide gulf cannot be spanned between a holy God and a sinful man by human effort, ingenuity, or will. A loving God Himself provided a way to span the divide by sending His son, Jesus Christ, who is "the way" to God (John 14:6). If there was an alternate means for man to have fellowship with a holy God, then there would be no need for His son, Jesus Christ, to come into the world. As His creation, God desired a relationship with man such that He sent His only begotten Son for us into this world to pay the penalty for sin and provide forgiveness, paving the way to growth in holiness and fellowship with Himself. Scripture declares that the wages of sin is death (Romans 6:23) and that Jesus died as a substitute for sinful man, taking upon Himself the punishment for the sin sufficient to pay the penalty of the sin of all mankind. As a sovereign God, Jesus conquered death and rose from the grave (Romans 1:4). Scripture says that whoever believes that Jesus died for our sins will be cleansed by the blood of Jesus Christ and declared positionally holy in the sight of God (Ephesians 1:7).

When we are forgiven and cleansed from all unrighteousness, God commands us to pursue holiness, which is the second element concerning holiness in scripture, that is, practical holiness. That is the reason for the command in 1 Peter 1:16 saying, "Be holy for I am holy." While we still contend with the sinful flesh, fighting temptation, and growing in sanctification, God empowers us through His word and the Holy Spirit to enable us to pursue it in a way that is acceptable to God. Thus, the seven instructions found in 1 Peter 1:13–18, when faithfully obeyed, will enable us to pursue holiness.

Let us therefore begin to unpack each of these instructions.

❧

*Chapter 1*

# Focus on the Thought Life

One of the first areas of focus regarding pursuing holiness should be our "thought life." Verse 13 of 1 Peter 1 states, "Therefore, preparing your minds for action," in the English Standard Version. God wants us to prepare our minds to be ready for the action He will direct us to do. The King James Version renders it as, "Wherefore gird up the loins of your mind." This imagery may be difficult to discern in our day, but the people who would have received this letter would have been able to. Men during the first century in the Middle East wore long, flowing robes that extended from their shoulders down to their feet. They also wore a rope around their waists. This acted as a belt. For routine activities like walking, they would let their long robes extend all the way down to their feet, but when they had to engage in strenuous physical activity like running or lifting/moving heavy objects, they would tuck the lower end of the robe around the waist. The idea was to remove any obstacle that would hinder successful completion of any activity. Another parallel verse that explains this thought is Hebrews 12:1. It states, "Therefore, since we are surrounded by so great a cloud of witnesses, let us also lay aside every weight, and sin which clings so closely, and let us run with endurance the race that is set before us." These verses clearly explain that we will not be successful in a running race if we are improperly clothed or have unnecessary weight on us as we compete. The unnecessary weight could cause us to slow down, and improperly worn attire causes the athlete to stumble and fall. As we run the race the Lord has set before us, we need to gird up the loins of our minds.

What does it mean to gird up the loins of the mind? It refers to what we are filling our minds with. If we fill our minds with sinful things, then this sin will hinder us in our walk with the Lord. Thought life is very important in our Christian life. We cannot fill our minds with sinful, lustful, and evil desires and follow a holy God wholeheartedly. What you fill your mind with will influence your actions.

There is a man of God that I respect a lot. He was a prayerful and faithful man. He was a very dynamic person and ministered as a youth pastor several years ago. We as a church could see the youth group grow in numbers and also mature in their walk with the Lord. I admired the way this man of God spoke, counseled the youth, and encouraged them with love and grace. God used him not only to minister to the youth but also mentored several people like me. He participated in several sports and coached many teams. No matter how competitive the games were or how the other team acted, his words were very kind, and I've never heard him say anything offensive. I was always amazed that though he was very passionate, he never cursed or yelled or said anything offensive.

This man of God disclosed in a sermon that as a young boy, he struggled with controlling his language! I was surprised knowing that this is a man of God under whom I learned a lot of things with regard to growing in the Lord and ministering among the youth. This was the last thing I expected him to have struggled with in the past. He went on to explain that when he was a young boy, he had a habit of using foul language and cursed a lot. Even though he came to the saving knowledge of Jesus Christ, he still struggled with this issue. When God called him to serve Him as a pastor and he went to college, he just couldn't control his language. This man of God was afraid he wouldn't be able to serve the Lord as his language would be a hindrance not only to the ministry but also in his walk with the Lord. Much as he tried, he couldn't stop this behavior. As he spent time in prayer, God showed him the issue. The music he heard, the programs he watched on television, and the friends he hung around with, they all influenced his language. These words were filling his mind and were having a sinful impact on him. Then he prayerfully decided to distance himself from those things. Knowing he couldn't control what people around him said, he focused on things he could control or change. He stopped watching programs that had this type of language. He stopped listening to music and hanging around friends who spoke this language. As he stopped feeding his mind with this type of language and curse words, his life began to change. He changed so much that even in the most provoking situations, he would never curse or use foul language. What you fill your mind with will ultimately influence your actions. God has given you His spirit and, through the Spirit, the wisdom to know right and wrong. If you fill your mind with God and His word, your actions will reflect that influence.

To illustrate further, in Matthew 5:27–28, Jesus Himself stated, "You have heard that it was said, 'You shall not commit adultery.' But I say to you that everyone who looks at a woman with lustful intent has already committed adultery with her in his heart." In the eyes of a holy God, the moment you look at someone with lustful eyes, you have already committed adultery. It is very important to examine our lives to see what we take in and what influences us. The God who made you and me is a holy God, and there is nothing hidden from Him, including our thoughts. It is written in 1 Samuel 16:7 that "the Lord sees not as man sees; man looks on the outward appearance, but the Lord looks on the heart." The creator of the universe knows you intimately. He can see what is filling your heart. The challenge is identifying what thoughts have been filling your heart. As you reflect on your life, the challenge is asking ourselves, "What are we filling our minds with? and "How are we preparing our minds to be consumed by God?" What will God see in your thought life? Are these the thoughts that please your Savior who created you in His own image and who came down and died on the cross for your sins?

Are there sins or a particular sin that you are constantly struggling with in your life? The first place is to examine yourself to see what you are filling your mind with. Scripture gives us clear instruction: "But be ye transformed by the renewing of your mind" (Romans 12:2). All of us are born in sin. When we come to the saving knowledge of Jesus Christ, we are made holy. But we still have the sinful nature in us. The sinful nature wants us to conform to the pleasures of the world (sin), but God wants our lives to be transformed by the renewal of the mind through setting our minds on the things that are above in heaven (Colossians 3:2). As long as your mind is thinking about the pleasures of sin that you are struggling with, this thinking will consume you. Instead, when you spend your time thinking about God and His kingdom, it will change your focus and you will be consumed with living a holy life that will bring glory to God.

Let the first thing that comes to mind when you wake up in the morning be having fellowship with God through reading His Word and through prayer. That will be a great start to your day. Ask God that the spirit of Truth should lead you to all truth throughout the day. Let bringing glory to God's name be the focus of your thought life and your prayers throughout the day. We know the life of John the Baptist. God gave a wonderful testimony about John the Baptist. The Bible calls him "a man sent from God" and "a witness about the Light (Christ)." John's life was such a reflection of who God is that people during his time mistook him to be Christ! John the Baptist had to clarify to the people during his time that he was not Christ. For the generations after him, the Bible clarifies that he was not the Light (Christ) but a witness of the Light. His life was all about humbling himself and serving God no matter what, even if it cost his life. The Scripture points that John the Baptist was a burning and shining lamp (John 5:35). He was burning for God from within. For our lives to be holy and our actions to reflect God's holiness, we need to have this burning passion within our minds to live a godly life and to bring glory to God before the actions can reflect them to the people around us.

As you come to the end of the chapter, the challenge for you and me is the examination of our thought life. Is there a burning desire for God and to live a godly life? Is it being consumed by the things that are above? To live a holy life, our minds have to be prepared for action first. If it is not consumed by things that are above, ask God for help. Only He can help you to have a pure thought life.

If you are struggling with a certain sin, ask God to examine your thought life. Examine yourself to see if the programs you watch, the friends that you hang out with, the books you read, the websites you surf, and the places you visit are consuming your mind with the pleasures of sin or promoting holiness in your life. Prayerfully make changes needed as the Word directs you.

## Chapter 2

# Focus on the Deed Life

God instructs us to then focus on our "deed life." Verse 13 of 1 Peter 1 also states "be sober." The New Living Translation presents it as "exercise self-control." This can be interpreted in at least two ways.

First, our lives should be free of sins that prevent us from pursuing holiness. When we hear the words *being sober*, addiction to alcohol or substance abuse is typically assumed as these things are what bring a person under sinful influence rather than being under the influence of God. These things do not promote holiness as they prevent us from using sound judgment and cause us to stumble in our walk with the Lord. These habits are sinful and cause a Christian to be vulnerable to engage in sinful behavior with either partial or no awareness or become a stumbling block to others. One of the examples that we see in Scripture is how Lot became the father to his two daughters' children when they made him drink wine excessively (Genesis 19: 30–38).

We, however, know that we are not to get drunk with wine as it is a sin but be filled with the Holy Spirit. But the list doesn't stop with exercising self-control over these two sins. Scripture states, "I appeal to you therefore, brothers, by the mercies of God, to present your bodies as a living sacrifice, holy and acceptable to God, which is your spiritual worship" (Romans 12:1). We need to understand that we are called to live a holy life and our bodies should be kept holy in the sight of the Lord. We need to cast off the works of darkness and put on the armor of light. We are instructed to walk properly as we are in the light and we are the children of light. We need to put on Lord Jesus Christ and "make no provision for the flesh, to gratify its desires" (Romans 13:12–14). The scripture clearly states that when we walk by the Spirit, we will not gratify the desires of the flesh. Some of the works of flesh presented in Scripture are sexual immorality, impurity, sensuality, idolatry, sorcery, enmity, strife, jealousy, fits of anger, rivalries, dissensions, divisions, envy, drunkenness, orgies, etc. But the fruits of the Spirit are love, joy, peace, patience, kindness, goodness, faithfulness, gentleness, and self-control. We cannot pursue the works of flesh as well as pursue holiness. When we live by the Spirit, only then will we not gratify the desires of the flesh (Galatians 5: 16–21).

Secondly, we need to make sure that the blessings God has given us do not become idols and prevent us from pursuing holiness. Our first priority in life must always be the pursuit of God and His glory. God's desire for us is to seek His kingdom and righteousness. Sometimes God may choose to bless us more than we can imagine or ask for, but we need to be faithful in loving and serving the Giver rather than the gifts. The lives of Joseph and Daniel are good examples. Joseph was faithful to God who elevated him to be the prime minister of Egypt and second-in-command to Pharaoh. Only in regard to the throne was Pharaoh greater than Joseph. At no point in his life does Joseph give priority to the blessings rather than the Giver. Similarly, Daniel was faithful to God, and God blessed Daniel. Daniel became the ruler over the province of Babylon and chief prefect over all the wise men of Babylon. Daniel was then promoted as the third ruler in the kingdom. Finally, Daniel was made one of the three high officials to whom the 120 satraps reported. Even Daniel, like Joseph, sought to live a holy life, and the blessings were secondary to him. Both these men of God continued to faithfully serve the Lord even though God blessed them with positions of influence and wealth. God may choose to bless some of His people with wealth or put them in high positions. God's expectation is that we will be good stewards of His blessings. We need to ensure that the blessings the Lord gives us bring glory to God and not become idols for us.

As an extreme example of faithlessness, we see Jehoshaphat, the king of Judah. He started his reign strong. Just like his father,

Asa, and forefather, David, he did what was right in the sight of the Lord. He sought God and walked in His commandments. The Lord blessed Jehoshaphat and established the kingdom in his hand. God gave him great riches and honor. The fear of the Lord fell upon all the kingdoms of the lands that were around Judah, and no one wanted war against Jehoshaphat. The Philistines and Arabians brought him tributes. He built fortresses and store cities. He had a strong army of 1.16 million men of valor. The Lord delivered Jehoshaphat when he committed the mistake of aligning with Ahab, a wicked king of Israel. Another time, the Moabites, Ammonites, and Meunites came to war against Judah, and the king experienced the deliverance from the Lord. Yet this king wanted more wealth and aligned with the wicked king Ahaziah in building ships to go to Tarshish. The Lord destroyed what he made, and the ships were wrecked. Sad end to a king the Lord blessed when his desire moved from serving the Lord to focusing on his earthly blessings and wealth.

We need to ask ourselves if the gifts and blessings God graciously grants us are being used to serve the Lord and bring glory to Him or being selfishly used for our own pleasures and are starting to consume us where we begin to desire to have more of these. Are these good blessings slowly moving our hearts that they are taking the place of God? For example, doing your job faithfully is a good thing. It is a blessing from God. God's desire for us is to work hard to take care of the family. We are commanded to obey our earthly masters with fear and trembling and do our jobs with a sincere heart as you would for Christ. We should thank God and do our job to the best of our ability so that God's name will be glorified through our good work. However, if a job becomes an obsession for us to the point that all we think about is work, then it is a problem. If we put in long work hours each day with the hope to grow in our careers only and it takes time away from being able to serve God, spend time with the family, and take care of your kids, then work has become an idol in our life even though it is a blessing. For us to be a disciple of God, we need to think only about God and serving Him. The rest of the things will fall in place. God will show us how to become a great husband/wife, father/mother, and worker. The rest of the things will fall in place when we get our priorities right.

To pursue holiness, first we need to exercise self-control over committing sins that control us and submit to the Holy Spirit to allow Him to control our lives. Secondly, we are called to exercise self-control over the blessings and not let them control and consume us; rather we must be consumed by God. As we come to the end of this chapter, the challenge is to examine our lives and ask God to show us the sins that are controlling us. He alone can provide victory, and there are several sources of help God has placed for various addictions. If you think you do not have addictions, examine to see if God is your first priority in life. Or are there blessings that are taking the place of God?

*Chapter 3*

# Focus on the Goal

G od wants us to focus on the hope He has given us that one day we will see Him. Verse 13 of 1 Peter 1 states, "Set your hope fully on the grace that will be brought to you at the revelation of Jesus Christ."

A farmer's hope is to harvest bountiful crops. I lived in Kansas for several years and had friends who were into farming. I knew that farming was hard work, but I didn't realize the amount of planning, preparation, and execution it took to be successful. To produce the crop, there is a lot of preparation and execution that has to happen. Depending on the crop and prior experience, the farmer would assess the timing to start the process so that the season would aid the growth of the plants and produce a great harvest. The farmer would take great care in selecting and procuring the best-quality seed. The farmer would prepare the field by plowing the soil, marking the layout of the field such that there is enough distance between the plants to grow. The seeds would be sown at optimal depth and spacing. Sufficient water is used to help with germination. The farmer has to pay constant attention to the plant growth. During the entire growth cycle till harvest is completed, the farmer is focused on the plants. The farmer must assess at every stage how the plants are doing. He is constantly monitoring the situation and takes appropriate actions to protect the plants and promote growth. The farmer must provide proper fertilization to provide nutrition to the plants, protect the plants from pests and insects, remove the weeds as needed, protect the produce from animals, etc. The farmer also selects the proper equipment and time for the harvest to maximize the produce. A farmer who sets his hope in producing excellent-quality crops will plan carefully as well as invest in resources and time to accomplish this goal to the best of his ability. The hope or the goal of producing good crops will consume the farmer's mind and drive his actions.

God wants us, as Christians, to set our hope fully on the coming of Jesus Christ and the grace that will be given to us. Nothing else that we set our hope on will help us in our pursuit of holiness. When we fully fix our hope on the coming of Jesus Christ, then will we focus only on those actions God will guide us to. The direction that comes from God when we abide in Him will result in actions that bear "much fruit" (John 15:5). This fruit is what matters for eternity at the coming of Jesus Christ or when we finish our course on earth.

One of the followers of Christ who has followed God whole-heartedly during his time on earth is Apostle Paul. He was mightily used for the glory of God. He traveled to many cities to proclaim God's word. He was instrumental in spreading the gospel, planted churches, and invested his life for the growth of the church and the gospel. He ministered to and encouraged so many Christians through his teachings, letters, and life. Paul wrote thirteen books in the Bible. Even after his death, God is using his testimony and writings to encourage us.

One of the many life statements Apostle Paul was inspired to write is, "For me to live is Christ, and to die is gain" (Philippians 1:21). This verse shows where Paul's heart was. Why did Paul count it as a gain to die? He counted it as a gain because that is what he was looking forward to all his life. His hope was in the coming of Lord Jesus Christ. He knew once his journey was completed on this earth, he would be in the presence of his Lord for eternity. Having this hope in him, he viewed his life on this earth as living for Christ.

This hope of seeing Jesus Christ influenced Paul so much that he went through a lot of pain and suffering for God's work. On five occasions, he received thirty-nine lashes at the hands of the Jews. On three occasions, he was beaten with rods. Once, he was stoned. He was shipwrecked three times. He faced dangers from rivers, robbers, his own people, and gentiles. He faced dangers in cities, the wilderness, the sea, and from false brothers. He went through sleepless nights, hunger and thirst, and the roughest of weather conditions. We all can see that Paul's thoughts and actions were centered around the hope he had. No matter how tough the circumstances were, no matter what price had to be paid, his life was centered around the blessed hope he had.

One of the verses often quoted from Scripture is written by Paul where he states, "I have fought a good fight, I have finished the race, I have kept the faith. Henceforth there is laid up for me the crown of righteousness, which the Lord, the righteous judge, will award to me on that Day, and not only to me but also to all who have loved his appearing" (2 Timothy 4:7–8). That was the Apostle Paul's focus toward the end of his life. Paul also knew that his time on earth was coming to a close. At this time, Paul wrote to let Timothy know that he loved the "appearing of Jesus Christ" and how this transformed his life to fight a good fight to finish his race successfully on this earth.

In this chapter, we understand that fully setting our hope on the coming of Jesus Christ will influence us to lead a holy life. If our hope is on the coming of Jesus Christ and also on something else like to have an excellent bank balance or great position in society, that is where our actions will drift us to. We will stumble in our walk with the Lord and not be able to lead a life pleasing to God.

The challenge for us from this chapter is to examine our lives to see if our hope is fixed on the coming of Lord Jesus Christ. What is our response to the question, "How much time did I spend the last few weeks meditating on the grace that will be brought to us on the revelation of Jesus Christ?" If our hearts are mindful about the coming of Jesus and how it would be in heaven with King Jesus seated high on the throne, then we have fully set our hope on the right thing. Can we truly say like Apostle Paul did that to die is gain because we will be in the presence of the Lord for eternity and will never be separated from Him? Is that hope truly driving our actions and activities in our lives? If we have a strong desire to live in this world for as long as possible with all the possible comforts and delay the end of our journey on this earth, then our hope is not on the right thing.

## Chapter 4

# Focus on Not Conforming to Worldly Passions

G od is asking us to continue to be vigilant in obeying His Word. Verse 14 of 1 Peter 1 states, "As obedient children, do not be conformed to the passions of your former ignorance." God counts us as "holy" at the moment we are brought to the saving knowledge of Jesus Christ. God traded our sin for holiness the moment we received the great gift of salvation. As part of God's saving grace, He has also given us practical instruction on how we are to live after our salvation. In this passage, we are instructed on how to pursue and continue to remain in holiness. First, our thoughts are to be filled with godly things and our thought life consumed by God. Second, our actions are also to be God centered to keep us from sin. Thirdly, our hope is set on the coming of Jesus Christ, which helps us to remain focused in our journey on this earth. When these things are true in our lives and we are being transformed, we can fully expect Satan to attack us so that we stumble in our walk with the Lord and fall into sinful traps.

In Scripture, we usually read about many that fall into temptation when life is peaceful. They lower their guard, stumble, and have been held up as examples for us of what not to do. The first husband and wife created by God are an example before us. After creation, God gave man dominion over the fish of the sea, birds of the heavens, and every living thing that moves on the earth. Every fruit was available for man to eat except the fruit from the tree of knowledge of good and evil. From the time the creative work of God was completed to the first temptation, man completed the exercise of giving names to all the livestock, birds of the heavens, and every beast. During this time, there were enough visits from the Lord that the husband and wife were able to recognize the presence of the Lord based on the sound of His walk. Man and woman had settled down.

It was during this time that the serpent came and tempted Eve. The serpent asked Eve, "Did God actually say, 'You shall not eat of any tree in the garden'?" Eve demonstrated that she knew the commandment of the Lord very clearly. Then the serpent followed up with a lie saying, "You will not surely die. For God knows that when you eat of it your eyes will be opened, and you will be like God, knowing good and evil." Then Eve made her assessment by looking at the tree. She found it to be visually good for food and a delight to her eyes and concluded that it would make her wise! The first sin was committed on the earth.

Another person who stumbled and committed a great sin was King David. David went through a lot of trials before his throne was established. He was faithful in whatever capacity the Lord put him in. As a shepherd boy, he faced difficulties from wild animals wanting to devour the sheep. David delivered the sheep from both the lions and the bears. When David heard a giant named Goliath defy the armies of the living God, he accepted the challenge at a time when no one in the Israelite army was willing to fight Goliath, and David defeated him.

David faced persecution from Saul multiple times. Saul was David's enemy continually. Twice Saul tried to unsuccessfully pin David with his spear. Saul tried to get David killed by the Philistines unsuccessfully. Saul tried one more time to pin David with his spear. David chose to run when Saul's men wanted to capture him at his home. David escaped from Naioth when Saul's messengers came thrice for him, finally Saul himself came for David. Saul not only killed eighty-five priests who helped David but the entire city of Nob including men, women, children, and infants along with the animals. Saul continued to pursue David through the wilderness of Ziph. David had his chance for vengeance at Engedi when Saul came after

David. David didn't kill Saul even though Saul was very vulnerable. Instead he told Saul how he spared his life and provided evidence. Saul didn't relent but continued to pursue David in the wilderness of Ziph. David could have killed Saul again at night when everybody was asleep. David spared Saul's life again and let King Saul know the following day that he didn't kill the king even though he had an opportunity. Even though David was a powerful man who could take on the wild animals, a giant, and soldiers, he did not try to kill or harm King Saul in any way as David knew Saul was God's anointed, and David waited for his time. David tore his clothes, lamented over the death of Saul, and put to death the person who killed King Saul.

David became king of Judah. It was followed by a battle at Gibeon with the king of Israel, Ish-bosheth. After David became king over all Israel, he fought battles against Philistines, Moabites, Zobahites, Syrians, and Ammonites.

This great man of God went through all these difficulties but was very faithful to God through all these circumstances. God blessed David, and he became a powerful king. It was when David was at peace and at rest that he was unguarded and was tempted. David was doing so well that he felt there was no need for him to be at war "in the spring of the year, the time when kings go out to battle." He wasn't actively engaged in the responsibility of leading his army in the battlefield. He was walking on the palace roof when he fell into temptation. This man of God who was walking in the ways of the Lord got drawn away by his lust for a woman during a careless time. His lust led him to commit adultery with a married woman who was the wife of a faithful soldier in his own army! David's attempts to cover up his sin by having Uriah go home and have relations with his wife so that the child can be deemed Uriah's failed; the faithful soldier Uriah refused to stay at home during the time of battle. David then committed a preplanned murder by abusing his authority and, in the process, got other innocent soldiers in his army killed along with Uriah to cover his sin. What a shame!

Most of the temptations come to us at a time when we are not on guard. Paul, a great apostle who is a fearless leader, went through a lot of pain and suffering for the gospel of God and made a wonderful comment. He was afraid of one thing and rightfully so. Paul states, "But I am afraid that as the serpent deceived Eve by his cunning, your thoughts will be led astray from a sincere and pure devotion to Christ" (2 Corinthians 11:3). When our thoughts as well as deeds are focused on God and our hope is on the coming of Christ, our lives will be in compliance with the word of God. Peter is warning us to expect temptations and pressure to conform to the passions of sin, leading us astray. Let us not be an example like Eve or David.

Usually these temptations come to us when we have gone through difficulties and have experienced relief. It is during those times of relief that we tend to lower our guard. Usually the temptation comes from familiar people and circumstances pressuring us to conform to the world rather than God's word. In this modern world, as we walk with the Lord, we should expect to have peer pressure to get us to conform to the passions of the world.

For several years, I have had the privilege of working in children and youth ministries in India and USA. Often I see children, when they come to the saving knowledge of Jesus Christ and grow in the Lord, whose lives begin to get transformed even at a young age, and they act very responsibly even at a very young age. God blesses them, and they do well at school. We see some changes in some kids when they go to college or high school, in some cases, when they go to middle school. To various degrees, we see some of them begin to act differently like not hanging out with the friends they grew up within church, becoming irregular in attending church, and also not seeming to love and be engaged in church activities like they used to in the past. We realize that our children begin to face peer pressure to fit into groups around them, and if they refuse to do so, they are mocked or accused of being narrow-minded for not fitting into the system/sins of the world.

This also happens at places of work too. We see temptations come to Christians in many ways in an attempt to have us conform to the world (sin). We need to understand that we are in the world but are not of the world. There are a lot of sins that gave us temporary pleasure in our sinful past, but when we trust God, we are commanded not to live in sin. However, we feel pressure to do things to conform to the model of the world even though we get clear direction from the Lord that it is not what God wants for us.

Even the nation of Israel wanted to fit into the model of "king" rulership of this world even though God clearly told them that His desire was to have the "judge" rulership model. God had been raising judges to rule over Israel for several generations. Every time the nation of Israel sinned, God would let the enemies defeat Israel and Israel be placed under tyranny. Unable to bear the pain, the Israelites would cry out to the Lord, and the Lord would raise a judge who would lead the nation of Israel to victory. Israelites would then faithfully serve the Lord till the judge died and then revert to sinning. This continued for several cycles. Once Joel and Abijah became judges, they themselves acted corruptly. The nation of Israel wanted to change the leadership to a king-ruled model to fix corruption. They could have asked God to take care of the corruption, and God would have addressed the issue of corruption.

God graciously provided Israel the consequences of having a king according to their desires. Their sons would have to work as horsemen, and some of them would have to work as laborers for the king. Their daughters would be cooks, bakers, and perfumers. The best of their fields, vineyards, and olive orchards would be given to the king's servants. A tenth of their grain and produce from vineyards would be given to the king's officers and servants. Their servants and young men would be taken to work for the king. A tenth of their livestock would be taken for the king. And finally, they would be the king's slaves (1 Samuel 8:10–22)! Even after God clearly told His desire and direction, the nation of Israel wanted a king who would judge them and go for battles "like all the nations." God let them have a king-led kingdom model per their desire. We know how that panned out for the Israelites. Among the three kings who ruled the kingdom of Israel, King Saul and King Solomon did not finish their courses well. The kingdom got split into Judah and Israel due to Solomon's sins. Most of the kings who ruled the nations of Judah were bad, and all the kings who ruled over Israel were bad.

The lesson from the story is that we are to obey God whether the circumstances are good or bad. The scripture is very clear when it states, "And we know that for those who love God all things work together for good, for those who are called according to His purpose" (Romans 8:28). God doesn't promise only good situations in our lives, but He promises that even through bad things, He will let them work for our good. Only trust in Him and do not conform to the world.

The warning for us is to be prepared to face pressure to conform to the worldly ways when we are well settled in our faith and things seem to be going well. We should never let our guard down; we should always be alert and expect to have pressure to conform to the passions of the world. If you think you do not have any pressures to conform to the worldly pleasures, examine your life to see if your walk with the Lord is strong or if are you compromising your stances when difficulties arrive. When was the last time you faced pressure?

🌱

*Chapter 5*

# Focus on Living in Reverent Fear

P eter is reminding us that we need to focus on living our lives on this earth in reverent fear of God. Verse 17 of 1 Peter 1 states, "conduct yourselves with fear throughout the time of your exile." Peter is emphasizing that God is impartial and has become our father the moment we came to the saving knowledge of Jesus Christ. For anyone brought into God's family, it is because God chose us even before the foundation of the world and adopted us as sons (Ephesians 1:4–5). So we need to understand that heaven is where we will be for eternity with our heavenly Father and that our time on earth is best described as temporary, as New American Standard Version says: *"During your time of stay on earth."*

To remain holy, we need to understand who our God is. It then puts things into perspective. I remember when I was in seventh grade, I won an award. The chief guest for the awards ceremony was the honorable minister for education. There were a lot of arrangements made prior to the event as someone very important was coming to attend. Few of us students who won the awards were given instructions and clear directions on what to do on the day of awards presentation as the chief guest was someone very important, so we had to follow certain protocols to ensure the safety of this important person and also be on our best behavior to impress this person. We were instructed where to stand in line, how to proceed when our name was called, how to receive the award from the chief guest, and how to exit after receiving the award. When the big day came, I was in awe of the security and arrangements made. The chief guest spent a few seconds to hand me the award and say "Congratulations." As a boy, I wondered how important and great this minister was that he had so much security and it was considered an honor that I could spend a few seconds with him.

The God we serve is a powerful God who is the creator of this universe. God created the heavens and the earth. He created light, separated waters, created dry land, made plants, the sun, moon, stars, animals, birds, and sea creatures by the word of His mouth. God made man in His own image and breathed life into man. The God we serve is eternal and sustains this universe.

God is infinitely wise and all-knowing. In this world, there are about 7.8 billion people. Our human mind cannot even remember the names of the people in our community, let alone try to remember the names of the people in our city or state or country or continent. God not only knows the names of all the peoples of the earth but also everything about every person, including the number of hairs on their head! Our church pastor was preaching a sermon, and he asked for a couple of volunteers to come to the front to illustrate the point on how difficult it is to count the number of hairs on a person's head. A boy and a girl came up. He first asked the girl to sit on a chair and face the congregation and asked the boy to count the number of hairs she had! The boy didn't know what to do. The pastor then had them reverse the roles. When the girl was asked to count the number of hairs on the boy's head, she didn't even know where to start counting from! On average, a person has a hundred thousand hairs on their head. God knows everything about the 7.8 billion people including the exact number of hairs on each person's head. Not only that but God also knows every person who lived on this earth in the past as well as every person that is going to be born in this world.

In the Old Testament, we read about the great men of God who saw a glimpse of the glory of God but not God in His strength. Moses, who spoke with God as a friend would speak face-to-face, had to hide in the cleft of the rock and got a glimpse of God but not His face. Adam and Eve heard the voice of God, but the Bible doesn't record them seeing Him. Children of God experienced the presence of the Lord as a pillar of clouds or a pillar of fire but not His face in His full glory.

On two occasions, there were men of God who saw God in a vision. In the Old Testament, Prophet Isaiah saw the Lord. Isaiah shares his vision where he saw the Lord seated upon a throne, high and uplifted. The train of His robe filled the temple. During the time of worship, the foundations of the temple were shaken and the whole house was filled with smoke. Isaiah's response was, "Woe is me! For I am lost; for I am a man of unclean lips, and I dwell in the midst of a people of unclean lips; for my eyes have seen the king, the Lord of hosts!" When Isaiah saw the Lord in all His splendor, his response was, "It's all over, I'm doomed for I am a sinful man."

In the New Testament, Disciple John was in the spirit on the Lord's day and got a glimpse of the glorified Christ in heaven. He saw Jesus as fully God and not a man anymore in His kingdom. King Jesus was in the midst of the seven golden lampstands. His face was shining like the sun in all its brilliance, hair like white wool, eyes like a flame of fire, feet like burnished bronze, and out of His mouth came a two-edged sword. In His right hand were seven stars, and He was clothed in a long robe with a golden sash. As He spoke, it thundered like the mighty ocean waves. When John saw King Jesus, all he could do was fall at the feet of King Jesus as if he was dead. John realized that after ascension, Jesus was no longer a human being like when He was with the disciples on earth. He was revealed as fully God (divine).

Often we forget how great our God is. We think of God as a human being who is a dear friend of ours and whose main responsibility is to take care of our needs and grant the desires of our hearts. We remember the thirty-three years when Jesus Christ came down to this earth and lived as a human being. We are tempted to think of the God of the Bible, who revealed Himself as Jesus Christ, as a great teacher, healer, and great friend who gave His life. We often forget that He is now ascended into heaven and is no longer a human being but fully God.

Are we living in reverent fear of God? All our activities are visible to God, and nothing is hidden from Him. We are not talking about a human of any significance like a mayor of a city or the governor of a state or the president of a nation, but we are talking about the most powerful authority that ever existed in history. This is God Almighty Himself, the creator and sustainer of the universe. Does the fact that one day we will stand before Him in person when He will judge us influence our actions? To live a holy life, we need to know who our God is and live in reverent fear of God knowing fully well that we are living on this earth for a very short period of time and will one day have to stand before this powerful God to give an account of our stewardship.

## Chapter 6

# Focus on the Price Paid for You

We need to remember the price paid for us to be brought into the kingdom of God. Verses 18 and 19 of 1 Peter 1 beautifully describe the price paid for us: "Knowing that you were ransomed from the futile ways inherited from your forefathers, not with perishable things such as silver or gold, but with the precious blood of Christ, like that of a lamb without blemish or spot." The price paid to place us into His family is substantial.

Over the years, the Lord has used many godly people to be an example and an encouragement to me. When I lived in Kansas, I was blessed to be part of a church where several families adopted children from all over the world who were in need of good homes. At that church, I got to observe one such God-fearing family. This family invited me to their house for lunch on one of the very first weeks after I started attending the church they were part of. We became very good friends and got to know one other very well. They faithfully served the Lord. One of the ministries the Lord put a burden in their hearts was to adopt children who were in need of good homes. They adopted kids from India, China, and other parts of the world. The couple invested in the lives of these children where they spent significant time, energy, and money to ensure that the kids were raised in the best possible conditions.

I remember very well when the couple shared the news that they were expecting their first baby. It was a joyous occasion, but I remember her comment that with this new addition to the family, they may not be able to adopt another baby like they intended to. So much was the couple's desire to adopt children into their family and show the children the love of God that God honored their desire and granted them the necessary resources to be able to adopt another baby even after they had their own child. Seeing the way these parents poured their lives into caring for these children, I used to think how blessed these kids are that they are now part of a God-fearing family where they will have a strong foundation in the Word, studies, sports, and become well rounded. When I saw adoptions take place in several families at this church, I could clearly see the love of God being manifested in works. I saw the prayers, planning, and preparations that occurred prior to adoption. I also saw the efforts put into raising the children with love, care, and discipline to the best of the parents' ability. I felt happy that the children adopted by families in this church were blessed to end up in such wonderful homes where prayers are offered continually and care is taken to develop the kids. If the adoptive parents went through this kind of sacrifice, it shows how important these children are in the eyes of the adoptive parents. As the kids grew up, they realized the sacrifices made by the adoptive parents. It showed how important they are to their parents and their parents' desire for them to do well. It encouraged the children to put their best effort to make their parents proud as they realized the cost paid to take care of them.

Sometimes we think about ourselves as somebody who is insignificant or of little value based on our income level, our house, or our position in society, forgetting how blessed we are that we are important in the eyes of our Lord and Redeemer. We might be a nobody in eyes of the world, but we are precious in the eyes of our Lord and Savior Jesus Christ. The sacrifice made by God to adopt us into His family is remarkable. First, the plan for our lives began even before the foundation of the world. God chose us before the foundation of this world to be holy and blameless before Him. He predestinated us for adoption as children into His family before the world was made!

Secondly, God paid the price for our sins on the cross. When we sinned, the wages of our sin is death. So we had to die for our sins. God loved us so much that when we were dead in our sins and transgressions, He became the substitute to take the punishment we deserved. There is no way man, by his own willpower or by determination, can reach God. There was no other way to reach God other than God's prescribed way, so Jesus became "the way" and not "one of the ways." There was no other door to God, so Jesus became "the door."

Almighty God, the creator, the sustainer of this universe, who dwells in the light no man can approach, took the punishment for sin on Himself. He left heaven and came down to this world in the form of a man. The whole purpose of coming into this world was to die for our sins. This was an excruciating and painful death He endured for us. He was arrested by the Jewish officers and Roman soldiers as a robber would be arrested even though He was completely sinless and innocent. The Creator was bound by these unlawful men. His own disciples deserted Him after His arrest. One of His disciples denied Him thrice. The men who were holding Jesus in custody were mocking Him as they beat Him. They blindfolded Him and kept asking Him, "Prophesy! Who is that struck you?" They said many other things against Him, blaspheming Him. He was struck by an officer as High Priest Annas interrogated.

Pilate and Herod, two different governors, reviewed the case but did not find anything wrong with Jesus. When Pilate was pressurized by the Jews to crucify Jesus, he just washed off his hands. Jesus was flogged, and the soldiers twisted together a crown of thorns and put it on His head. They mocked Him, saying, "Hail, king of the Jews!" The rulers scoffed at Him stating He saved others; "Let Him save himself, if He is the Christ of God, his chosen one!" They finally crucified Him on the cross with two other thieves. One of the thieves who hung on the cross also rebuked Jesus stating, "Are you not the Christ? Save yourself and save us." They cast lots for His garments. As Jesus hung on the cross, giving up His life for all the people of the world, He felt thirst. A sponge dipped in sour wine and attached to a hyssop branch was held to His mouth. One of the soldiers pierced His side even after He died. Being God, He rose from death on the third day and defeated sin. He finished the task and then ascended into heaven.

At any point during the trial or crucifixion as Jesus experienced extreme pain and agony, He could have stepped down from the cross and destroyed the persecutors. He did not do it not because He was helpless but because His love paid the penalty. He knew the price needed to be paid so that we can be redeemed and become His children again!

Third, even the decision we made to confess our sins to God, believing in the work done on the cross where Jesus died in our place and gave us salvation as a gift, and the decision to accept Jesus into our lives did not happen on our own. It was God who gave us the wisdom and insight to understand the mystery of His will. When God enlightens the eyes of our hearts, then are we saved. So we should bring nothing except our sin to the transaction where our sins were forgiven, and we will be redeemed.

You and I are so valued in the sight of the Lord that an all-powerful God made plans for us even before He laid the foundations of the world. When we went astray due to our sins, God loved us so much that He gave His own life as a substitute for our punishment. God is the one who opened our eyes of understanding so that we can come to the saving knowledge of Jesus Christ. We should not forget the price paid for us. This plan and sacrifice by God should motivate us to live a life He has chosen for us, that is to be holy and blameless before Him.

Do we continually remember His sacrifice for us? Do the sacrifice and cost paid influence every decision we make and every action we do?

*Chapter 7*

# Focus on Brotherly Love

This is a very important aspect that God wants us to focus on. Verse 22 of 1 Peter 1 states, "love one another earnestly from a pure heart." In the prior chapter, we see that we were redeemed from our fruitless ways not with perishable things like such as silver or gold but with the precious blood of Christ. You are so precious in the eyes of the Lord that He left His heaven's glory, came down to this world in the form of a man, and died a painful and cruel death on Calvary's hill when He hung upon the cross so that you can be added to God's family. So is every person that is added into God's family. Each of them is very important in the sight of the Lord that He gave His life for them to add them to His heavenly kingdom.

God loves His people very much. When God's people are oppressed and cry out to Him, He listens to them. Saul was persecuting the church. He was breathing threats and murder against the disciples of the Lord. He got letters from the high priest to arrest God's children in Damascus and bring them to Jerusalem. As Saul was on his way to Damascus, a light from heaven shone around him. Saul fell to the ground. It was Jesus who appeared and spoke to Saul. The first statement that came from the Lord is, "Saul, Saul, why are you persecuting me?" Saul didn't know who was speaking to him at that time and asked the Lord, "Who are you, Lord?" Then the Lord gave a wonderful answer to Saul. He said, "I am Jesus, whom you are persecuting." That is how important His children are to Him. Any harm against the children of God is harm done against King Jesus Himself. We need to make sure that we love God's children just like we love God.

When Jesus Christ was in this world, one of the parables He shared was Jesus being the true vine. In this parable, God the Father is the vinedresser, Jesus is the true vine, and we are the branches. The expectation is that every branch has to bear fruit. A branch that is no longer part of the vine gets withered away and cannot bear any fruit. These withered-away branches are of no use and are typically gathered and thrown into fire, where they get burned. Likewise, we cannot have fruitful lives without abiding in Jesus and His words abiding in us, which is the expectation of God the Father. Just as God the Father loved the Son, so has the Son loved us. The Son has kept the Father's commandments, and so He abides in God the Father's love. God the Son instructs us to abide in His love. If we keep the commandment of God the Son, we will abide in His love too. The commandment that Jesus gives us is to love one another as He loves us. Jesus goes on to call us His friends because He has shared with us everything He heard from God the Father. Jesus says greater love has no one than this, that someone lay down his life for his friends. He demonstrated His love for us by laying down His life for us who He called His friends. He has given us these instructions so that we will love one another.

If you have experienced the agape (sacrificial) love of God, it will make you love the Lord wholeheartedly, and this love will also translate to philia (brotherly) love. When Jesus Christ was in this world, He was asked what the great commandment in the Law is. In Jesus's response, He doesn't state one command but two. Jesus states that you shall love the Lord your God with all your heart and with all your soul and all your mind. This is the great and first commandment. He then goes on to state that there is a second commandment, that you shall love your neighbor as yourself.

When we come to the saving knowledge of Jesus Christ, we have experienced agape love where God laid down His life for us. We are now part of the Lord's family, and every believer in God becomes a brother or sister in Christ. God gives us clear instructions in 1 John on what He expects from us. God clearly states that His expectation is that our love for one another should not just be mere words but should translate to deeds and in truth. Our love for each other should be so great that we are even willing to lay down our lives for each other!

As I reflect on my life, I am so thankful God has placed in my life godly men and women who have exhibited this character. When my dad was alive, he loved God so much that his love for God translated to love for God's children who were brothers and sisters in Christ. His love for brothers and sisters in Christ was evident to me when I saw both my parents spend time in prayer four times a day, pleading with God for the needs of the people God placed in their lives. When dad was promoted to glory, so many of our family members, church family members, and friends shared with us how Dad cared for them personally and was involved in encouraging and uplifting them as they went through difficult times in their lives.

On numerous occasions, great men and women of God that God placed in our lives have loved our family so much that they invested and poured out their lives to encourage us and ensure that we grew in the Lord. As we were going through very tough situations in life, the way the Lord used these people to minister to us was a testimony and an example of how to love God's people. I remember one particular occasion when a trial lasted for several months. The Lord used our home fellowship group to minister to us. The genuine love and care our home fellowship members had for us made us open up and share the exact struggles we were going through. They prayed for us continually not only during the time of home fellowship but also in their personal prayers. Every time we would meet for our home fellowship, they would follow up to see how we were doing with this particular issue. We would discuss how the Lord encouraged us at times through particular portions of Scripture, and we would also share the progress. They continued to pray until the Lord answered our prayers and the issue was resolved!

The challenge for you and I is having received the agape love of God, is it translating to philia love? When was the last time we were able to minister to a brother or sister God placed in our lives? As we reflect back on the last several weeks, what would our Maker say about our love to Him and His children?

# Conclusion

The God who has saved us when we were dead in our sins and transgressions is a sovereign King of kings, Lord of lords, and God of gods; He is a great, mighty, and awesome God who is holy. In the passage that we meditated on, the central theme is in verse 16 where it states, "You shall be holy, for I am holy." We know that holiness is a character we are called to pursue.

Knowing who God is and understanding the standard God wants us to follow, it would seem almost impossible to do what God is commanding us to do. Holiness is important in our lives because the Scripture states that without holiness, no one will see God. There is no way man, by his own willpower and determination, can become holy. God came down to this world and paid the price for our sin when He died a cruel death on Calvary's hill when He hung on the cross. God is the one who opened our eyes so that we can turn away from darkness to light and from the power of Satan to God. God chose us as the first fruits to be saved through sanctification by the Spirit and belief in the truth. We received forgiveness of sins and a place among those who are sanctified by placing their faith in God. Praise be to God as He has given us His holiness when we came to the saving knowledge of Jesus Christ.

We are made holy by God, and it is His will that we continue to live in holiness. We need to preserve our own bodies in holiness and honor. We should not be living in the passions of lust. God is the one who will continue to sanctify us through His Word. Praise be to God that in this passage, God is giving us help on seven aspects He wants us to focus on with His help.

First, we must let our minds be filled with godly things and be consumed by God. As we get filled up with the Holy Spirit, we will be prepared to face temptations. Secondly, we must live a focused life where our sole attention is on God and everything else becomes either secondary or something we avoid. Thirdly, we must live our lives keeping the goal in front of us, understanding the purpose for which the Lord has put us in the world and living in accordance to it.

As we do these three things, our lives will continue to be transformed into the image of Jesus Christ. We will then see strong opposition from the devil. Fourth, we need to make sure we understand our transformation. We will be tempted by the sins that gave us sinful and temporary pleasure in the past. Our friends or people around us will try to put peer pressure on us to conform to do sinful things. We should not conform to the passions of our former past.

Fifth, we need to live in reverent fear of God. We need to understand who is asking us to be holy. This is the creator of the universe who maintains it. In this is an all-powerful God who exists from eternity to eternity and in whose presence we can't even stand. Sixth, we need to experience the love of God. We need to understand how much this all-powerful God cares for us and has blessed us. Great men and women of God who powerfully served the Lord were pure in their hearts. They had a balance of the love of God and the reverent fear of the Living God. Your life cannot be effective unless you experience both and give importance to both aspects.

Finally, our love for God has to translate to brotherly love. Each believer belongs to the same family: the family of God. We need to understand how important each person is in the sight of the Lord and treat our brothers and sisters in Christ the same way.

Prayerfully ask the Lord for His help. Remember these seven practical aspects that God has instructed us to do so that we will continue to remain in the holiness that God has called us to. Now may the God of peace Himself sanctify you completely, and may your whole spirit and soul and body be kept blameless at the coming of our Lord Jesus Christ.

# About the Author

Samson Namala was born into a conservative Christian family in Hyderabad, India. He lived in India for over twenty years where he came to the saving knowledge of Jesus Christ, began serving the Lord, and then moved to the United States where he continued in the ministry. He had the opportunity to learn the Word of God from many godly men from these two continents.

In the past three decades, Samson served in several ministries among children, youth, and adults. He learned that the Word of God works with the same power and has the same impact in transforming peoples' lives despite culture, place, or tradition. God has given us commands, principles, and instructions in His Word that transcend time or tradition.